CVC Words

What are CVC words?

CVC stands for "Consonant Vowel Consonant".

A CVC word is a word that is made up of a consonant, vowel and consonant letter sequence.

For example, CAT is a CVC word. Because it follows the consonant - vowel - consonant letter sequence.

Instructions

1) Trace the dotted CVC words.
2) Write the words in the blank lined space below each word.
3) Trace the dotted sentences. These sentences contain the corresponding CVC words.
4) Write the sentences in the blank lined space below each sentence.

Bonus Fun: Get free hilarious coloring pages of farting pokemon. Download, print and start coloring!

Visit www.alexsmith101.com/bonus

Words ending with "ab"

cab — I took a cab.

cab cab cab cab cab

I took a cab

Words ending with "ab"

lab — He is in the lab.

lab lab lab lab lab lab

He is in the lab

Words ending with "ab"

tab | I paid the tab.

tab tab tab tab tab

I paid the tab

Words ending with "ad"

dad | My dad is at work.

dad dad dad dad dad

My dad is at work

Words ending with "ad"

had — I had milk after dinner.

had had had had had

I had milk after dinner.

Words ending with "ad"

mad — I saw a mad dog.

mad mad mad mad

I saw a mad dog.

Words ending with "ad"

sad | Why are you sad?

sad sad sad sad sad

Why are you sad?

Words ending with "ag"

bag | Sam packed his bag.

bag bag bag bag bag

Sam packed his bag.

Words ending with "ag"

lag — He always lags behind.

lag lag lag lag lag lag

He always lags behind.

Words ending with "ag"

tag — Mia saw the price tag.

tag tag tag tag tag

Mia saw the price tag.

Words ending with "am"

dam — They have built a dam.

dam dam dam dam

They have built a dam.

Words ending with "am"

ham — Make a ham sandwich.

ham ham ham ham

Make a ham sandwich.

Words ending with "am"

jam — He ate bread and jam.

jam jam jam jam jam

He ate bread and jam.

Words ending with "an"

can — Sarah can swim.

can can can can can

Sarah can swim.

Words ending with "an"

fan — Paul is a baseball fan.

fan fan fan fan fan

Paul is a baseball fan.

Words ending with "an"

man — You are a kind man.

man man man man

You are a kind man.

10

Words ending with "an"

van — We hired a van.

van van van van van

We hired a van.

Words ending with "ap"

cap — I have lost my cap.

cap cap cap cap cap

I have lost my cap.

Words ending with "ap"

map — Look at the map.

map map map map

Look at the map.

Words ending with "ap"

nap — Linda is taking a nap.

nap nap nap nap nap

Linda is taking a nap.

Words ending with "as"

gas — My car is out of gas.

gas gas gas gas gas

My car is out of gas.

Words ending with "at"

bat — I have a baseball bat.

bat bat bat bat bat

I have a baseball bat.

Words ending with "at"

cat — David has a white cat.

cat cat cat cat cat cat

David has a white cat.

Words ending with "at"

fat — The hen was very fat.

fat fat fat fat fat fat

The hen was very fat.

Words ending with "at"

mat Nancy bought a mat.

mat mat mat mat mat

Nancy bought a mat.

Words ending with "ax"

wax I bought a wax candle.

wax wax wax wax wax

I bought a wax candle.

Words ending with "eb"

web — The spider spun a web.

web web web web

The spider spun a web.

Words ending with "ed"

bed — She went to bed.

bed bed bed bed bed

She went to bed.

Words ending with "ed"

red — I have a red pencil.

red red red red red

I have a red pencil.

Words ending with "ed"

fed — Have you fed the cat?

fed fed fed fed fed

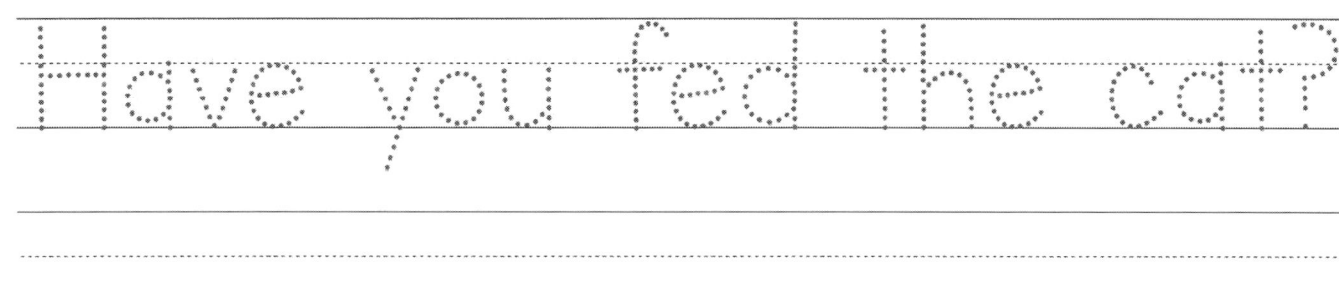

Have you fed the cat?

Words ending with "eg"

beg — I beg your pardon.

beg beg beg beg beg

I beg your pardon.

Words ending with "eg"

leg — The cow broke its leg.

leg leg leg leg leg leg

The cow broke its leg

Words ending with "em"

gem — Mom wore a red gem.

gem gem gem gem

Mom wore a red gem.

Words ending with "en"

hen — The hen laid two eggs.

den den den den den

The hen laid two eggs.

Words ending with "en"

men | Those men are chefs.

men men men men

Those men are chefs.

Words ending with "en"

pen | May I use your pen?

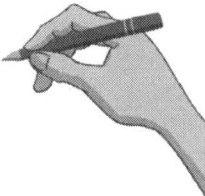

pen pen pen pen pen

May I use your pen?

Words ending with "en"

ten | Ten years have passed.

ten ten ten ten ten

Ten years have passed.

Words ending with "es"

yes | Yes, I can do it.

yes yes yes yes yes

Yes, I can do it.

Words ending with "et"

get | Don't get mad at me.

get get get get get

Don't get mad at me.

Words ending with "et"

met | I met him at the park.

met met met met

I met him at the park.

Words ending with "et"

pet — Ryan has a pet parrot.

pet pet pet pet pet

Ryan has a pet parrot.

Words ending with "et"

wet — The grass is wet.

wet wet wet wet wet

The grass is wet.

Words ending with "ib"

rib — He has broken a rib.

rib rib rib rib rib rib

He has a broken rib.

Words ending with "id"

did — What did you eat?

did did did did did did

What did you eat?

Words ending with "id"

kid | The kid is playing.

kid kid kid kid kid kid

The kid is playing.

Words ending with "id"

rid | I got rid of the books.

rid rid rid rid rid rid

I got rid of the books

Words ending with "ig"

big — I saw a big tree.

big big big big big big

I saw a big tree.

Words ending with "ig"

dig — The soil is hard to dig.

dig dig dig dig dig dig

The soil is hard to dig

Words ending with "ig"

| pig | Dad owns a pig firm. |

pig pig pig pig pig pig

Dad owns a pig farm.

Words ending with "im"

| him | I gave him a candy. |

him him him him him

I gave him a candy.

Words ending with "im"

dim The light began to dim.

dim dim dim dim dim

The light began to dim.

Words ending with "im"

rim The cup has a red rim.

rim rim rim rim rim

The cup has a red rim.

Words ending with "in"

bin — Put the box in the bin.

bin bin bin bin bin bin

Put the box in the bin.

Words ending with "in"

kin — Are you kin to Gary?

kin kin kin kin kin kin

Are you kin to Gary?

Words ending with "in"

pin | Pin the pages together.

pin pin pin pin pin pin

Pin the pages together.

Words ending with "in"

sin | It is a sin to waste food.

sin sin sin sin sin sin

It is a sin to waste food

Words ending with "in"

win — We want to win.

win win win win win

We want to win.

Words ending with "ip"

hip — My hip is hurting.

hip hip hip hip hip hip

My hip is hurting.

Words ending with "ip"

lip — Amy bit her lower lip.

lip lip lip lip lip lip lip

Amy bit her lower lip.

Words ending with "ip"

tip — I gave the porter a tip.

tip tip tip tip tip tip

I gave the porter a tip.

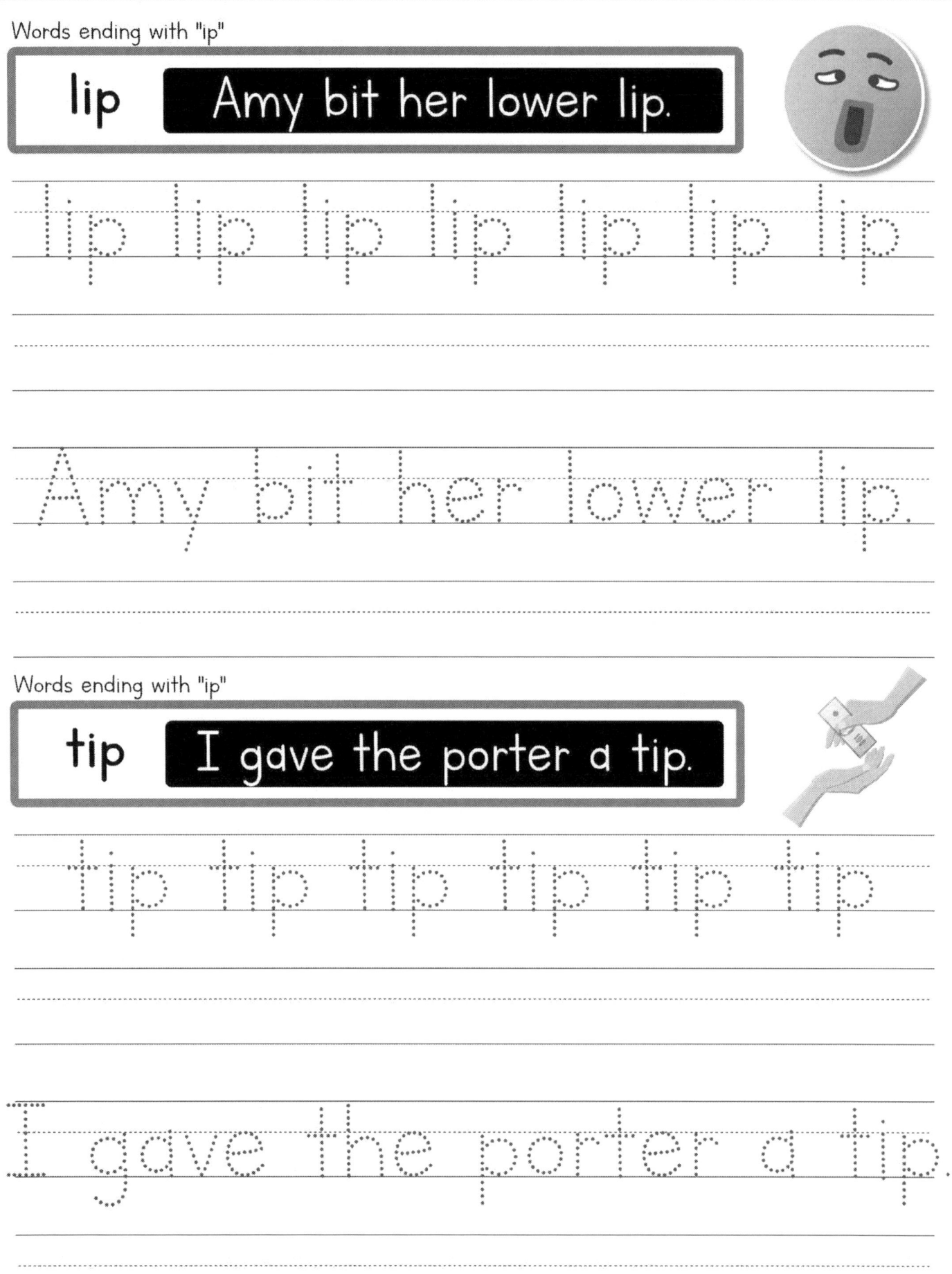

Words ending with "it"

fit — Carl is healthy and fit.

fit fit fit fit fit fit fit

Carl is healthy and fit.

Words ending with "it"

hit — Alex hit a home run.

hit hit hit hit hit hit hit

Alex hit a home run.

Words ending with "it"

pit | The pit is 6 feet deep.

pit pit pit pit pit pit

The pit is 6 feet deep.

Words ending with "it"

sit | Sit down and relax.

sit sit sit sit sit sit sit

Sit down and relax.

Words ending with "ix"

| fix | Mom will fix the clock. |

fix fix fix fix fix fix fix

Mom will fix the clock.

Words ending with "ix"

| mix | Mix the egg with flour. |

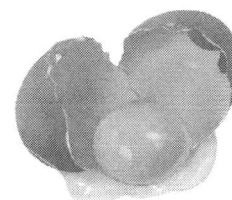

mix mix mix mix mix

Mix the egg with flour.

Words ending with "ix"

six — It was ten past six.

six six six six six six

It was ten past six.

Words ending with "ob"

job — Arthur has a new job.

job job job job job job

Arthur has a new job.

Words ending with "ob"

mob | A mob gathered here.

mob mob mob mob

A mob gathered here.

Words ending with "ob"

rob | He tried to rob me.

rob rob rob rob rob

He tried to rob me.

Words ending with "od"

God — May God bless you.

God God God God God

May God bless you.

Words ending with "od"

nod — She gave me a nod.

nod nod nod nod nod

She gave me a nod.

Words ending with "od"

| **rod** | He has a fishing rod. |

rod rod rod rod rod

He has a fishing rod.

Words ending with "og"

| **dog** | The dog is barking. |

dog dog dog dog dog

The dog is barking.

Words ending with "og"

fog We got lost in the fog.

fog fog fog fog fog

We got lost in the fog.

Words ending with "og"

hog The hog ran away.

hog hog hog hog hog

The hog ran away.

Words ending with "og"

| log | Put a log on the fire. |

log log log log log log

Put a log on the fire.

Words ending with "om"

| mom | Mom bought a puppy. |

mom mom mom mom

Mom bought a puppy.

Words ending with "op"

| cop | My brother is a cop. |

cop cop cop cop cop

My brother is a cop.

Words ending with "op"

| pop | Julia loves pop music. |

pop pop pop pop pop

Julia loves pop music

Words ending with "op"

top — He climbed to the top.

top top top top top

He climbed to the top

Words ending with "ot"

dot — Always dot your i's.

dot dot dot dot dot

Always dot your i's.

Words ending with "ot"

got — I got up at 5 o'clock.

got got got got got

I got up at 5 o'clock.

Words ending with "ot"

not — It is not cold today.

not not not not not

It is not cold today.

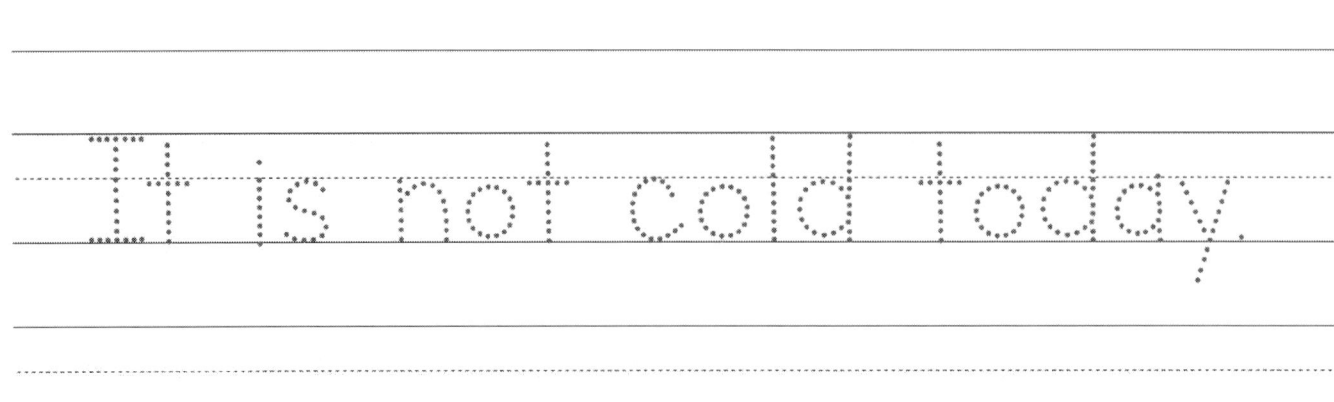

Words ending with "ot"

pot — He made a pot of tea.

pot pot pot pot pot

He made a pot of tea.

Words ending with "ox"

box — Please open the box.

box box box box box

Please open the box.

Words ending with "ox"

fox — A fox is a wild animal.

fox fox fox fox fox fox

A fox is a wild animal.

Words ending with "ub"

cub — The tiger cub is cute.

cub cub cub cub cub

The tiger cub is cute.

Words ending with "ub"

rub | Diana rubbed her eyes.

rub rub rub rub rub

Diana rubbed her eyes.

Words ending with "ub"

tub | He sat in a hot tub.

tub tub tub tub tub

He sat in a hot tub.

Words ending with "ud"

bud | The rose is in bud.

bud bud bud bud bud

The rose is in bud.

Words ending with "ud"

mud | Joe fell into the mud.

mud mud mud mud

Joe fell into the mud.

Words ending with "ug"

dug — He dug out the weeds.

dug dug dug dug dug

He dug out the weeds.

Words ending with "ug"

hug — Joe gave Roy a hug.

hug hug hug hug hug

Joe gave Roy a hug.

Words ending with "ug"

jug The jug was half full.

jug jug jug jug jug jug

The jug was half full.

Words ending with "ug"

mug I drank a mug of juice.

mug mug mug mug

I drank a mug of juice.

Words ending with "um"

gum — Lisa is chewing gum.

gum gum gum gum

Lisa is chewing gum.

Words ending with "um"

sum — The sum of 2 and 3 is 5.

sum sum sum sum sum

The sum of 2 and 3 is 5.

Words ending with "un"

fun — It was a lot of fun.

fun fun fun fun fun

It was a lot of fun.

Words ending with "un"

nun — Helen lived like a nun.

nun nun nun nun nun

Helen lived like a nun.

Words ending with "un"

run — Jacob can run fast.

run run run run run

Jacob can run fast.

Words ending with "un"

sun — Ice melts in the sun.

sun sun sun sun sun

Ice melts in the sun.

Words ending with "up"

pup | He gifted me a pup.

pup pup pup pup pup

He gifted me a pup.

Words ending with "up"

cup | My cup is empty.

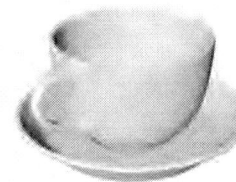

cup cup cup cup cup

My cup is empty.

Words ending with "us"

bus | I go to school by bus.

bus bus bus bus bus

I go to school by bus.

Words ending with "ut"

but | Jerry tried but failed.

but but but but but

Jerry tried but failed.

Words ending with "ut"

cut — Kelly cut the rope.

cut cut cut cut cut

Kelly cut the rope.

Words ending with "ut"

hut — He lived in a tiny hut.

hut hut hut hut hut

He lived in a tiny hut.

CVCC Words

What are CVCC words?

CVCC stands for "Consonant Vowel Consonant Consonant".

A CVCC word is a word that is made up of a consonant, vowel, consonant and consonant letter sequence.

For example, FISH is a CVCC word. Because it follows the (C)(V)(C)(C) letter sequence.

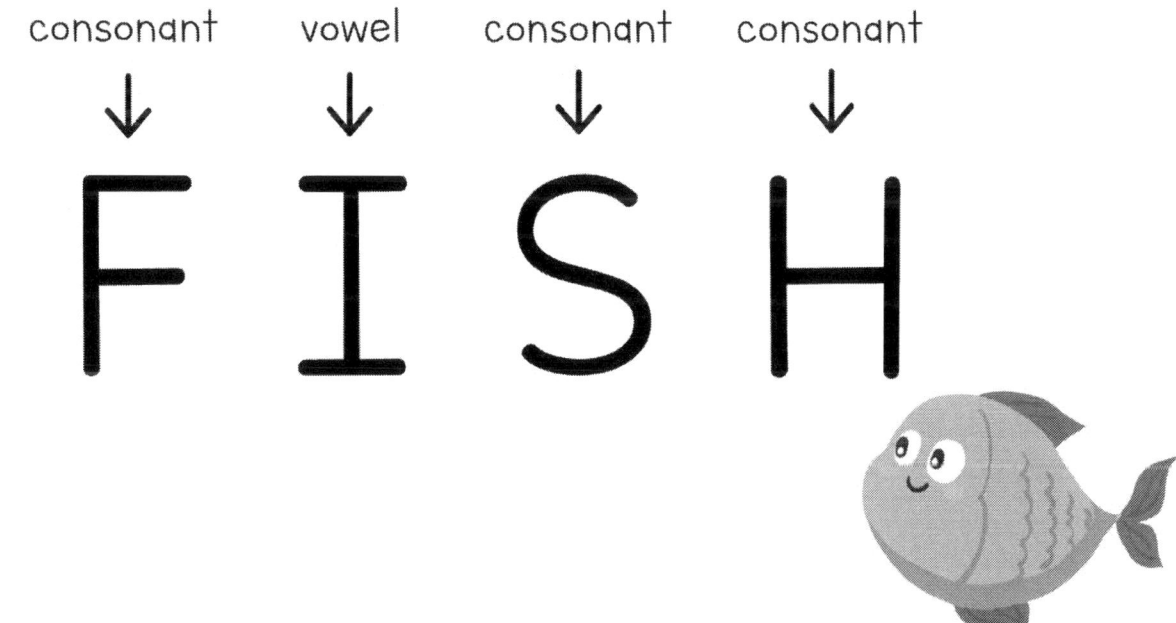

Words ending with "ack"

back | She came back home.

back back back back

She came back home.

Words ending with "ack"

pack | Brian will pack his bag.

pack pack pack pack

Brian will pack his bag.

Words ending with "ack"

rack — The rack has six hooks.

rack rack rack rack

The rack has six hooks.

Words ending with "ack"

sack — The toy was in a sack.

sack sack sack sack

The toy was in a sack.

Words ending with "ath"

bath — Did you take a bath?

bath bath bath bath

Did you take a bath?

Words ending with "ath"

math — He is good at math.

math math math math

He is good at math.

Words ending with "ash"

cash — I paid cash for the toy.

cash cash cash cash

I paid cash for the toy.

Words ending with "ash"

dash — Add a dash of salt.

dash dash dash dash

Add a dash of salt.

Words ending with "ash"

mash | Mash the potatoes.

mash mash mash mash

Mash the potatoes.

Words ending with "ash"

rash | Don't scratch the rash.

rash rash rash rash

Don't scratch the rash.

63

Words ending with "eck"

deck — He stood on the deck.

deck deck deck deck

He stood on the deck.

Words ending with "eck"

neck — She tickled my neck.

neck neck neck neck

She tickled my neck.

Words ending with "ick"

kick | Nathan kicked the ball.

kick kick kick kick

Nathan kicked the ball.

Words ending with "ick"

pick | Pick up the trash.

pick pick pick pick

Pick up the trash.

Words ending with "ick"

sick — Heather has been sick.

sick sick sick sick sick

Heather has been sick

Words ending with "ish"

fish — I caught two big fish.

fish fish fish fish fish

I caught two big fish

Words ending with "ish"

wish — I wish to be a doctor.

wish wish wish wish

I wish to be a doctor.

Words ending with "ock"

lock — The lock is broken.

lock lock lock lock lock

The lock is broken.

Words ending with "ock"

rock | He went rock climbing.

rock rock rock rock

He went rock climbing.

Words ending with "ock"

sock | Her socks are black.

sock sock sock sock

Her socks are black

Words ending with "uck"

buck — You owe me ten bucks.

buck buck buck buck

You owe me ten bucks.

Words ending with "uck"

duck — The duck flew away.

duck duck duck duck

The duck flew away.

Words ending with "uck"

luck — Goodbye and good luck.

luck luck luck luck

Goodbye and good luck.

Words ending with "uck"

tuck — Tuck your shirt in.

tuck tuck tuck tuck

Tuck your shirt in.

Words ending with "ush"

gush — I felt a gush of wind.

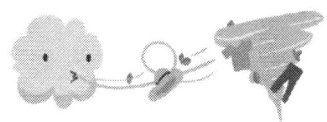

gush gush gush gush

I felt a gush of wind.

Words ending with "ush"

hush — Hush! They will hear us.

hush hush hush hush

Hush! They will hear us.

Words ending with "ust"

must — We must learn English.

must must must must

We must learn English.

Words ending with "ond"

pond — The pond is full of fish.

pond pond pond pond

The pond is full of fish.

CCVC Words

What are CCVC words?

CCVC stands for "Consonant Consonant Vowel Consonant".

A CCVC word is a word that is made up of a consonant, consonant, vowel and consonant letter sequence.

For example, SWIM is a CCVC word. Because it follows the (C)(C)(V)(C) letter sequence.

consonant	consonant	vowel	consonant
↓	↓	↓	↓
S	W	I	M

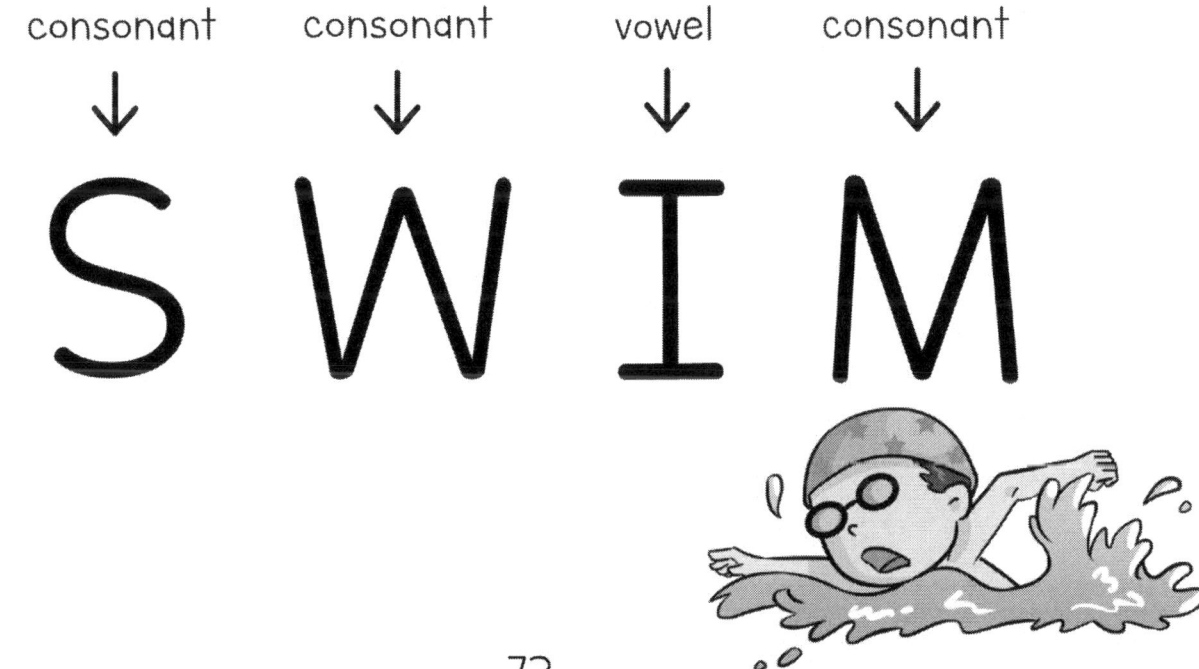

Words ending with "ab"

crab — The crab has two claws.

crab crab crab crab

The crab has two claws

Words ending with "ab"

grab — Grab the umbrella.

grab grab grab grab

Grab the umbrella

Words ending with "ag"

drag — He dragged his bag.

drag drag drag drag

He dragged his bag.

Words ending with "ag"

flag — Bryan raised the flag.

flag flag flag flag flag

Bryan raised the flag

Words ending with "am"

slam — Don't slam the door.

slam slam slam slam

Don't slam the door.

Words ending with "im"

swim — I know how to swim.

swim swim swim swim

I know how to swim.

Words ending with "an"

clan The whole clan was here.

clan clan clan clan clan

The whole clan was here.

Words ending with "an"

plan We agreed to the plan.

plan plan plan plan plan

We agreed to the plan.

Words ending with "ap"

clap — We gave her a big clap.

clap clap clap clap clap

We gave her a big clap.

Words ending with "ap"

slap — I wanted to slap myself.

slap slap slap slap slap

I wanted to slap myself.

Words ending with "ap"

trap — The fox fell into a trap.

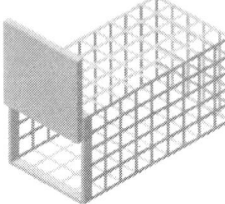

trap trap trap trap trap

The fox fell into a trap.

Words ending with "at"

chat — I had a chat with Tom.

chat chat chat chat

I had a chat with Tom.

Words ending with "at"

flat Paul lay flat on the floor.

flat flat flat flat flat

Paul lay flat on the floor.

Words ending with "ed"

fled She fled from the room.

fled fled fled fled fled

She fled from the room.

Words ending with "ed"

shed — He built a bicycle shed.

shed shed shed shed

He built a bicycle shed.

Words ending with "en"

then — What happened then?

then then then then

What happened then?

Words ending with "en"

when | When is school over?

when when when when

When is school over?

Words ending with "ep"

step | Don't step on my toes.

step step step step

Don't step on my toes.

Words ending with "im"

slim Andrew is tall and slim.

slim slim slim slim

Andrew is tall and slim.

Words ending with "im"

trim The lawn needs a trim.

trim trim trim trim

The lawn needs a trim.

Words ending with "im"

swim — Can rabbits swim?

swim swim swim swim

Can rabbits swim?

Words ending with "in"

chin — Keep your chin up.

chin chin chin chin

Keep your chin up.

Words ending with "in"

skin — She has a smooth skin.

skin skin skin skin skin

She has a smooth skin.

Words ending with "in"

thin — Don't skate on thin ice.

thin thin thin thin thin

Don't skate on thin ice.

Words ending with "in"

twin — I have a twin brother.

twin twin twin twin

I have a twin brother.

Words ending with "ip"

clip — Clip the pages together.

clip clip clip clip clip

Clip the pages together.

Words ending with "ip"

ship — I saw a cargo ship.

ship ship ship ship ship

I saw a cargo ship.

Words ending with "ip"

slip — Be careful not to slip.

slip slip slip slip slip

Be careful not to slip.

Words ending with "ip"

| trip | Dad cancelled his trip. |

trip trip trip trip trip

Dad cancelled his trip.

Words ending with "it"

| spit | Spit your gum out. |

spit spit spit spit spit

Spit your gum out.

Words ending with "og"

clog Debris can clog the pipe.

clog clog clog clog clog

Debris can clog the pipe.

Words ending with "og"

frog The frog was croaking.

frog frog frog frog

The frog was croaking.

Words ending with "op"

chop | Eric likes to chop wood.

chop chop chop chop

Eric likes to chop wood.

Words ending with "op"

shop | I went to the gift shop.

shop shop shop shop

I went to the gift shop.

Words ending with "op"

drop — I felt a drop of rain.

drop drop drop drop

I felt a drop of rain.

Words ending with "op"

stop — This is the bus stop.

stop stop stop stop

This is the bus stop.

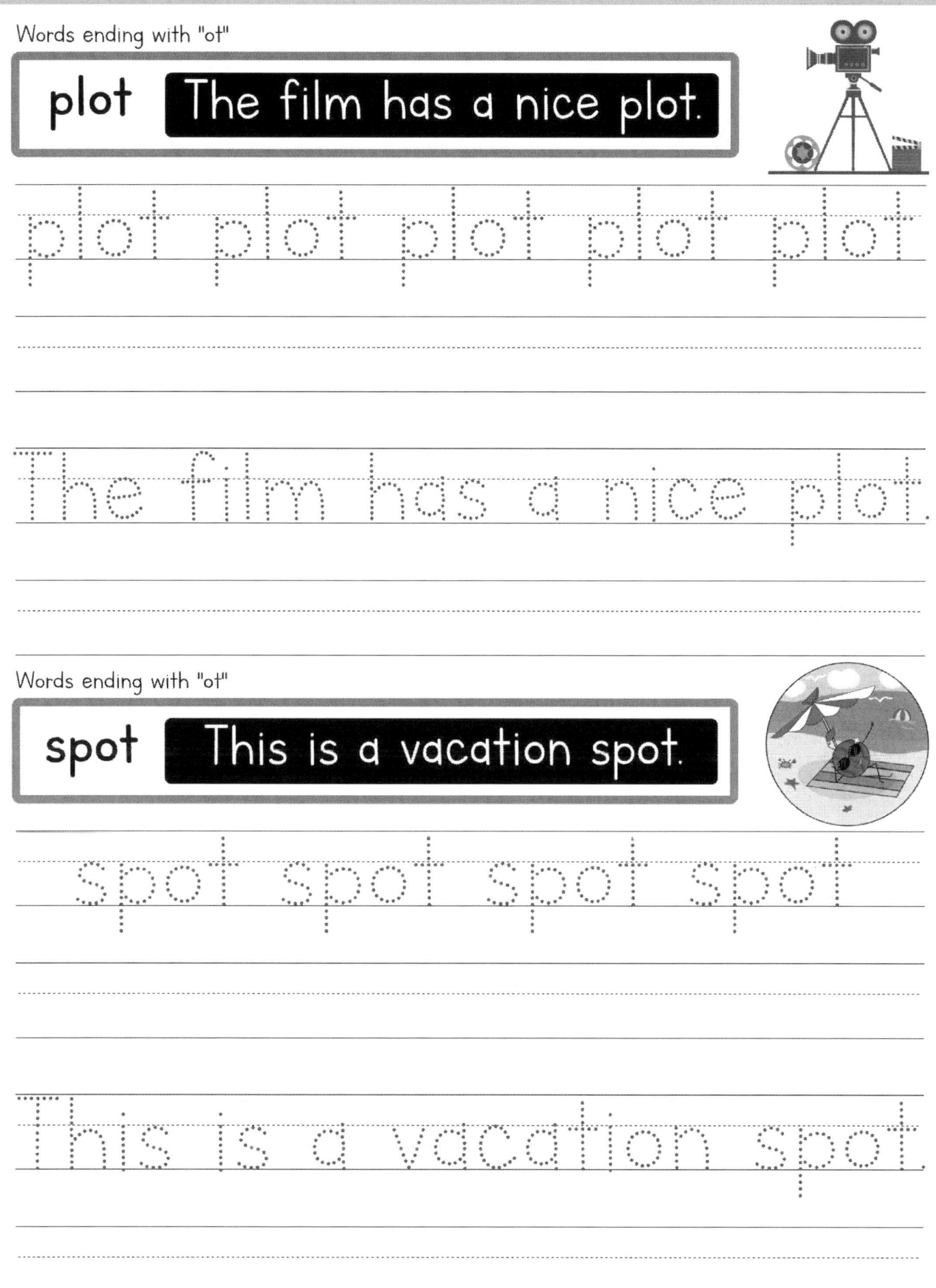

Words ending with "ub"

club I joined a baseball club.

club club club club

I joined a baseball club.

Words ending with "ug"

plug Please plug the leak.

plug plug plug plug

Please plug the leak.

Words ending with "um"

drum — Lisa is beating a drum.

drum drum drum drum

Lisa is beating a drum.

Words ending with "ut"

shut — Mom shut the window.

shut shut shut shut

Mom shut the window.

Words ending with "us"

plus — Two plus four is six.

plus plus plus plus plus

Two plus four is six.

Words ending with "id"

skid — The car went into a skid.

skid skid skid skid skid

The car went into a skid.

5 Letter CVC Words

Words ending with "ack"

black We have a black horse.

black black black black

We have a black horse

Words ending with "ack"

snack We stopped for a snack.

snack snack snack

We stopped for a snack

Words ending with "ack"

quack We heard a loud quack.

quack quack quack

We heard a loud quack

Words ending with "ack"

track Ruth lost track of time.

track track track track

Ruth lost track of time

Words ending with "ash"

crash The tree fell with a crash.

crash crash crash

The tree fell with a crash.

Words ending with "ash"

flash A bright flash went off.

flash flash flash flash

A bright flash went off.

Words ending with "ash"

smash Smash the door open.

smash smash smash

Smash the door open.

Words ending with "eck"

check He will check the map.

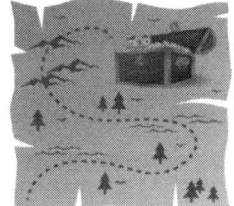

check check check

He will check the map.

Words ending with "eck"

wreck — That is a ship wreck.

wreck wreck wreck

That is a ship wreck.

Words ending with "ell"

dwell — We dwell in Dallas.

dwell dwell dwell dwell

We dwell in Dallas.

Words ending with "ell"

shell The snail has a shell.

shell shell shell shell

The snail has a shell.

Words ending with "ick"

brick The wall is built of brick.

brick brick brick brick

The wall is built of brick.

104

Words ending with "ick"

quick — I had a quick breakfast.

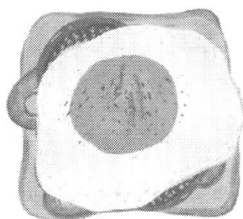

quick quick quick quick

I had a quick breakfast.

Words ending with "ick"

trick — I learned a new trick.

trick trick trick trick

I learned a new trick

105

Words ending with "ock"

clock Did the alarm clock ring?

clock clock clock clock

Did the alarm clock ring?

Words ending with "ock"

flock I keep a flock of geese.

flock flock flock flock

I keep a flock of geese.

Words ending with "ock"

stock — Chairs are out of stock.

stock stock stock stock

Chairs are out of stock.

Words ending with "uck"

pluck — Did you pluck the leaf?

pluck pluck pluck pluck

Did you pluck the leaf?

Words ending with "uck"

stuck I got stuck in the mud.

stuck stuck stuck stuck

I got stuck in the mud.

Words ending with "uck"

truck We unloaded the truck.

truck truck truck truck

We unloaded the truck.

Words ending with "ush"

brush — Brush your teeth.

brush brush brush

Brush your teeth.

Words ending with "ush"

flush — Please flush the toilet.

flush flush flush flush

Please flush the toilet.

Words ending with "umb"

thumb Jack raised his thumb.

thumb thumb thumb

Jack raised his thumb.

Words ending with "ght"

night I ate rice last night.

night night night night

I ate rice last night.

Made in the USA
Monee, IL
21 February 2021